What is that?
How did it get under my bed?

Is it wet?
Yes, it is wet.
How did it get under my bed?

2

Is it a mess?
Yes, it is a mess.
How did it get under my bed?

Is it red?
Yes, it is red.
How did it get under my bed?

 4

Does it have legs?
Yes, it has legs.
How did it get under my bed?

Is it my pet?
Yes, it is my pet.
How did my pet get under my bed?

6

Is it Rex?
Yes, it is Rex.
How did Rex get under my bed?

Rex is all wet.
He is a big mess!